This alphabet and numbers coloring book belongs to_______________________

____

____

____

____

____

____

Aa

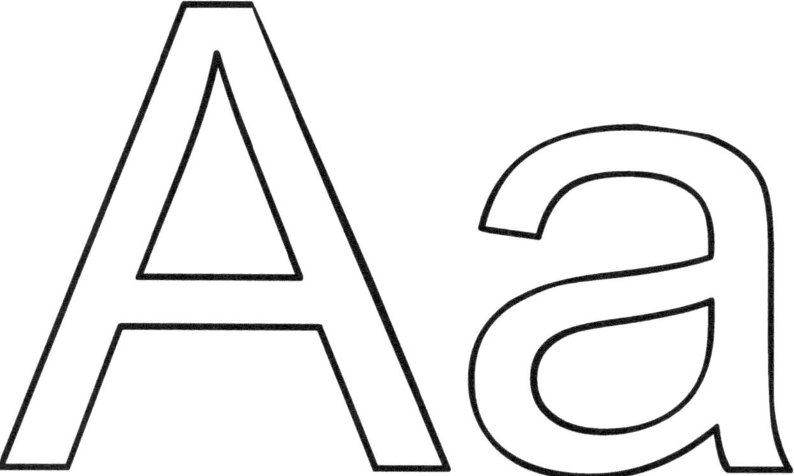

Trace the letters with a pencil

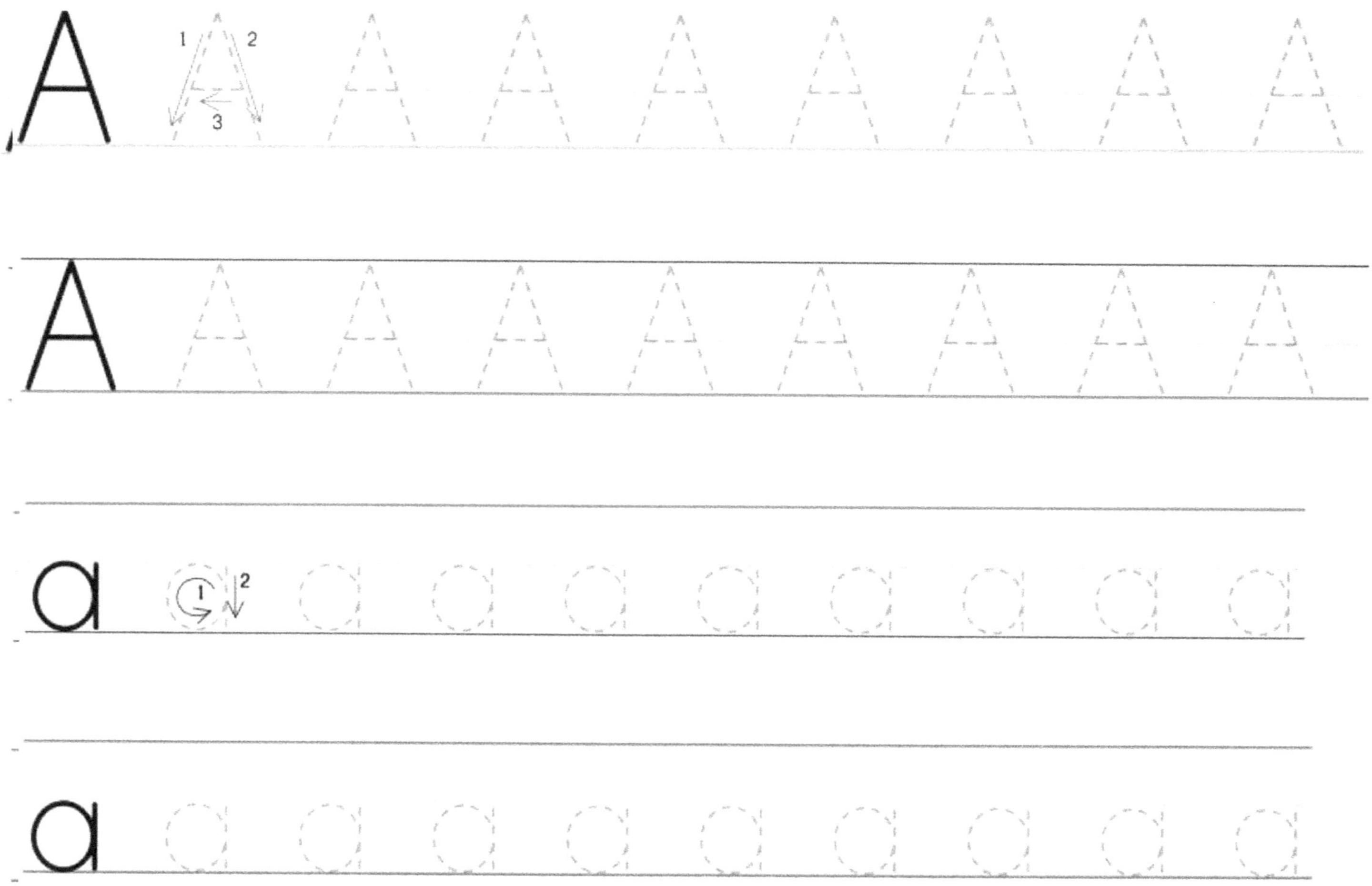

Apple ___________

Trace the letters with a pencil

Bird ___________________

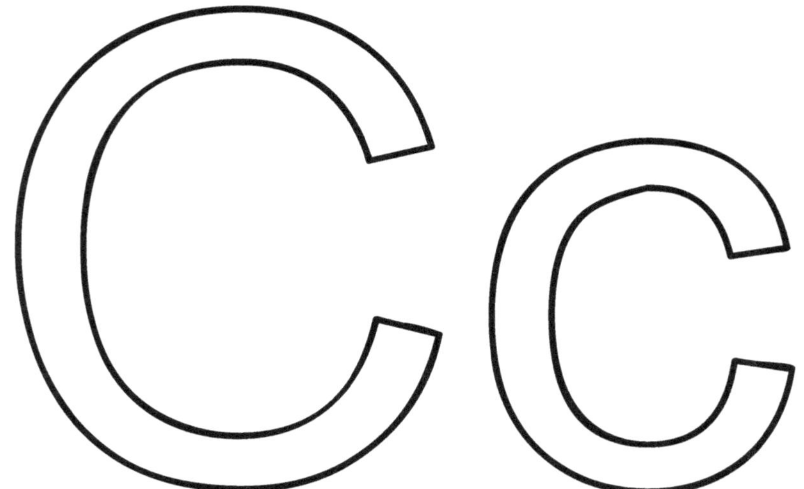

Trace the letters with a pencil

C C C C C C C C

C C C C C C C C

C C C C C C C C

C C C C C C C C

Cat

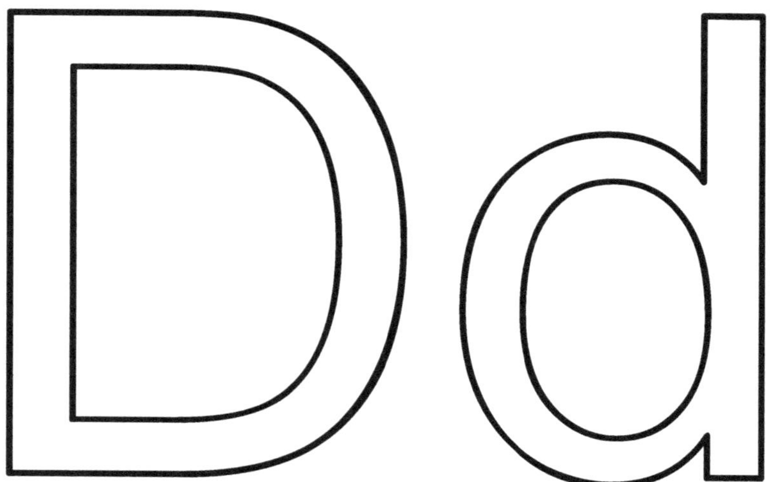

Trace the letters with a pencil

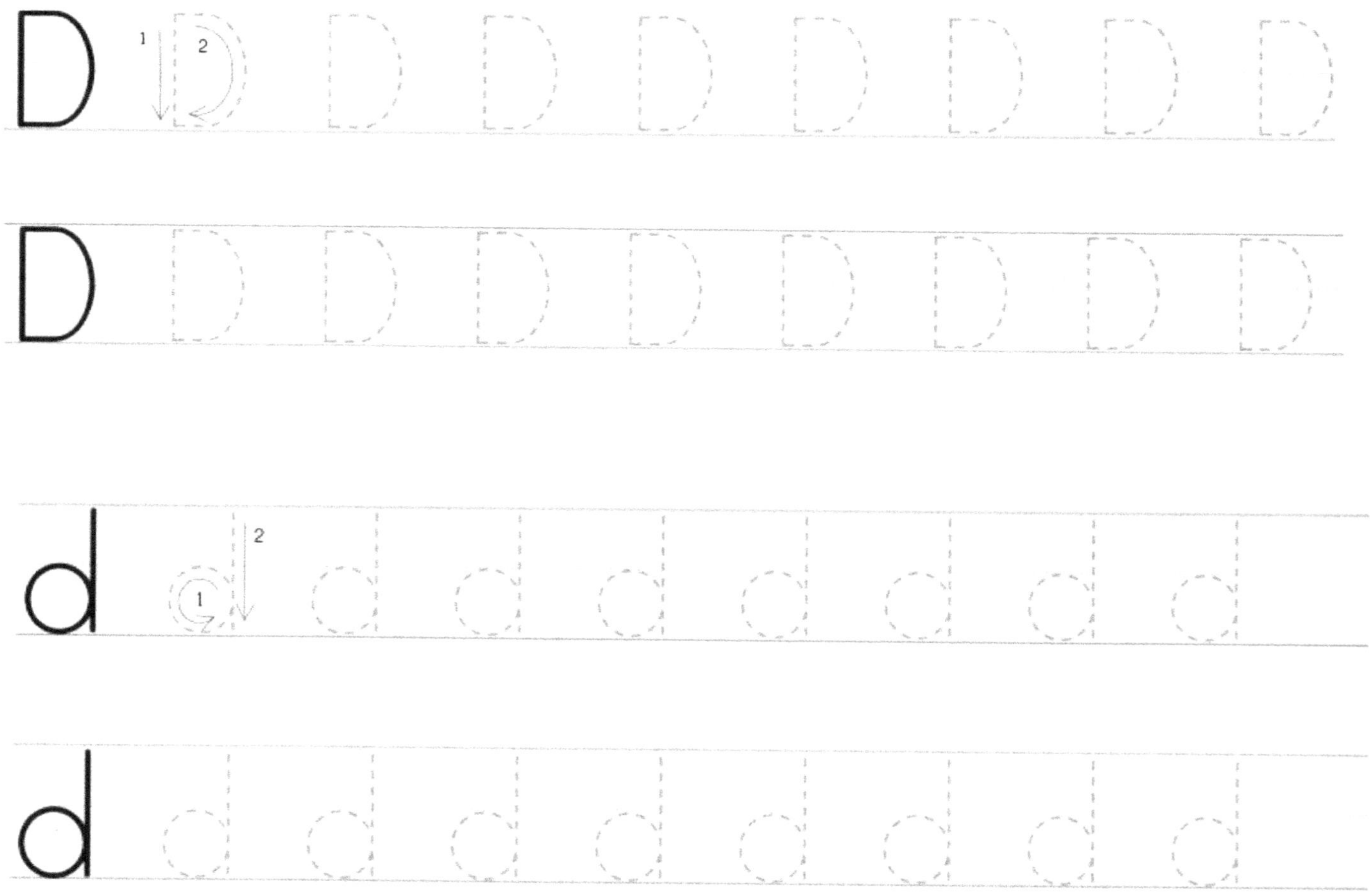

D D D D D D D D D D D D

D D D D D D D D D D D D

d d d d d d d d

d d d d d d d d

Dog _______________

Ee

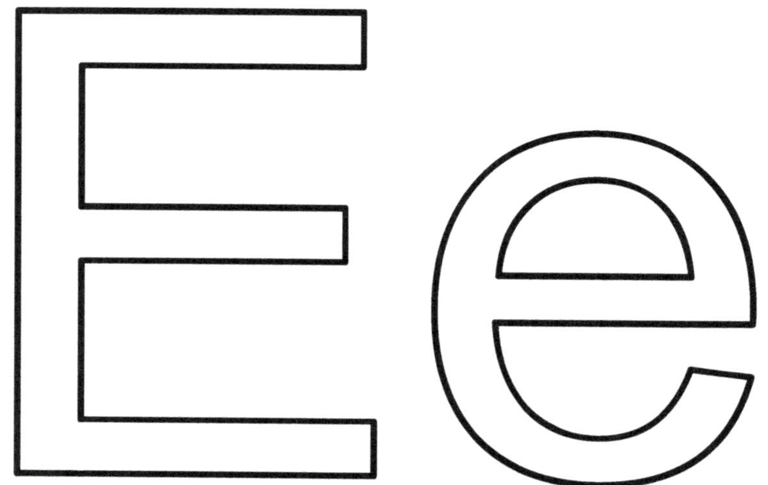

Trace the letters with a pencil

E

E

e

e

Elephant ———

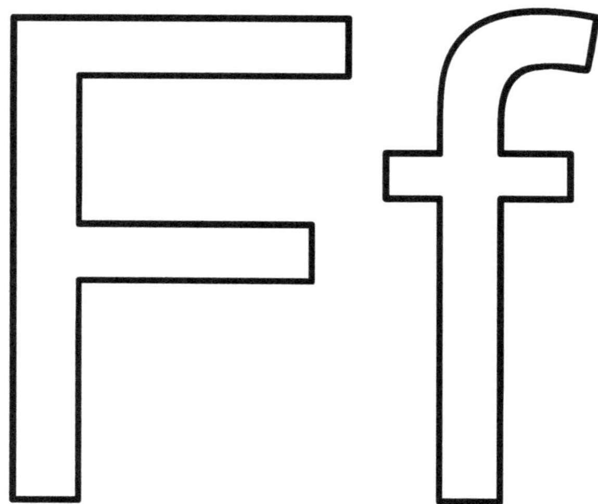

Trace the letters with a pencil

Fox ________________

Trace the letters with a pencil

G

G

g

g

Grapes ————————

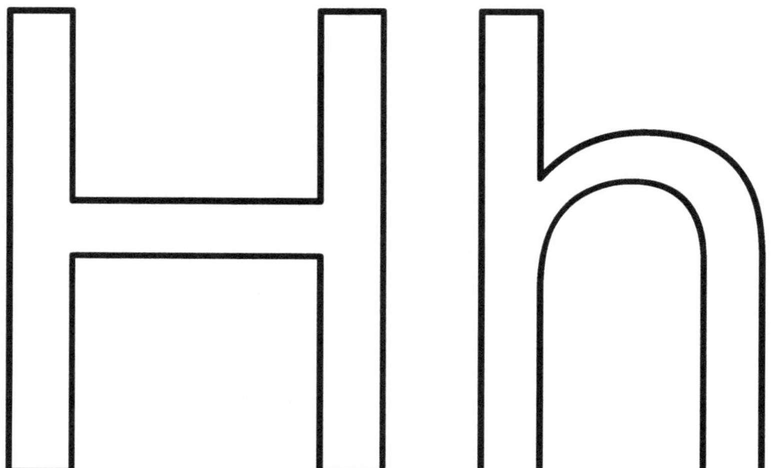

Trace the letters with a pencil

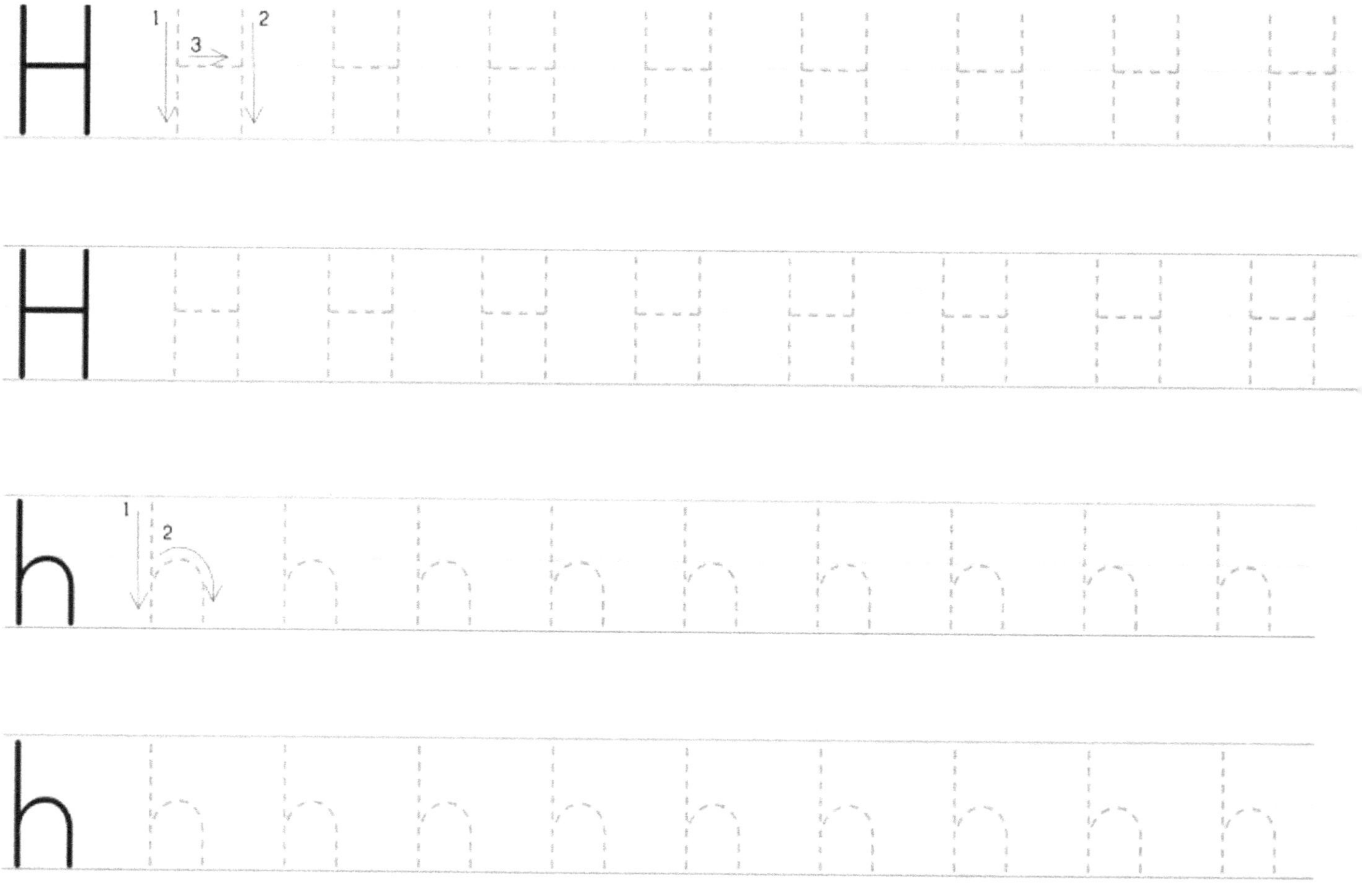

Horse ___________

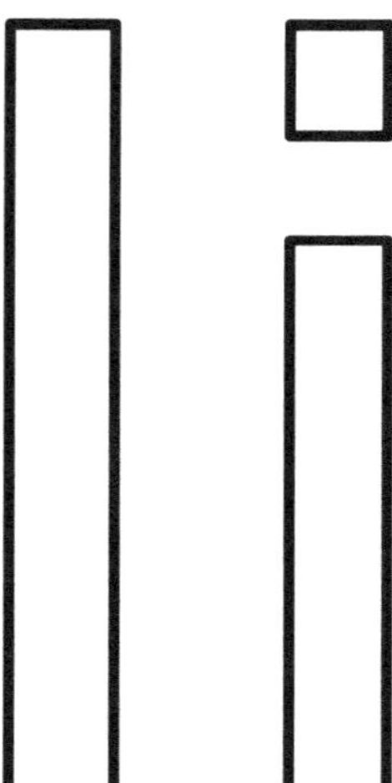

Trace the letters with a pencil

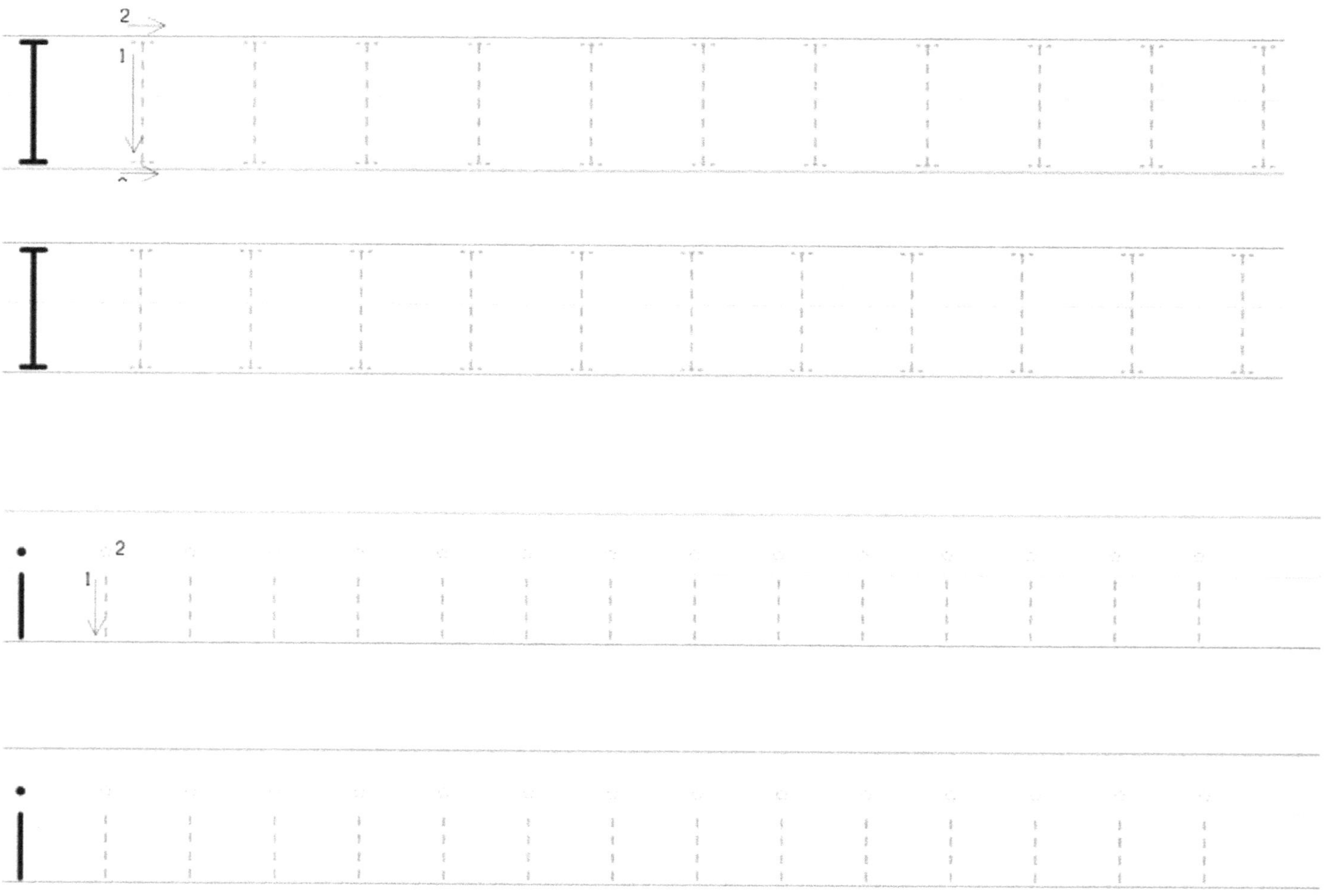

Ice Cream ——————

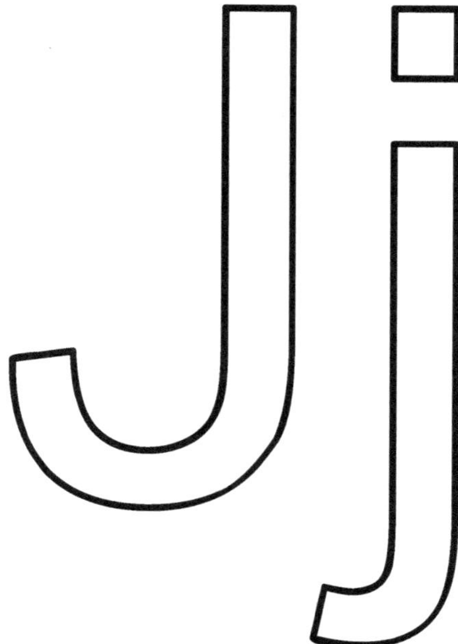

Trace the letters with a pencil

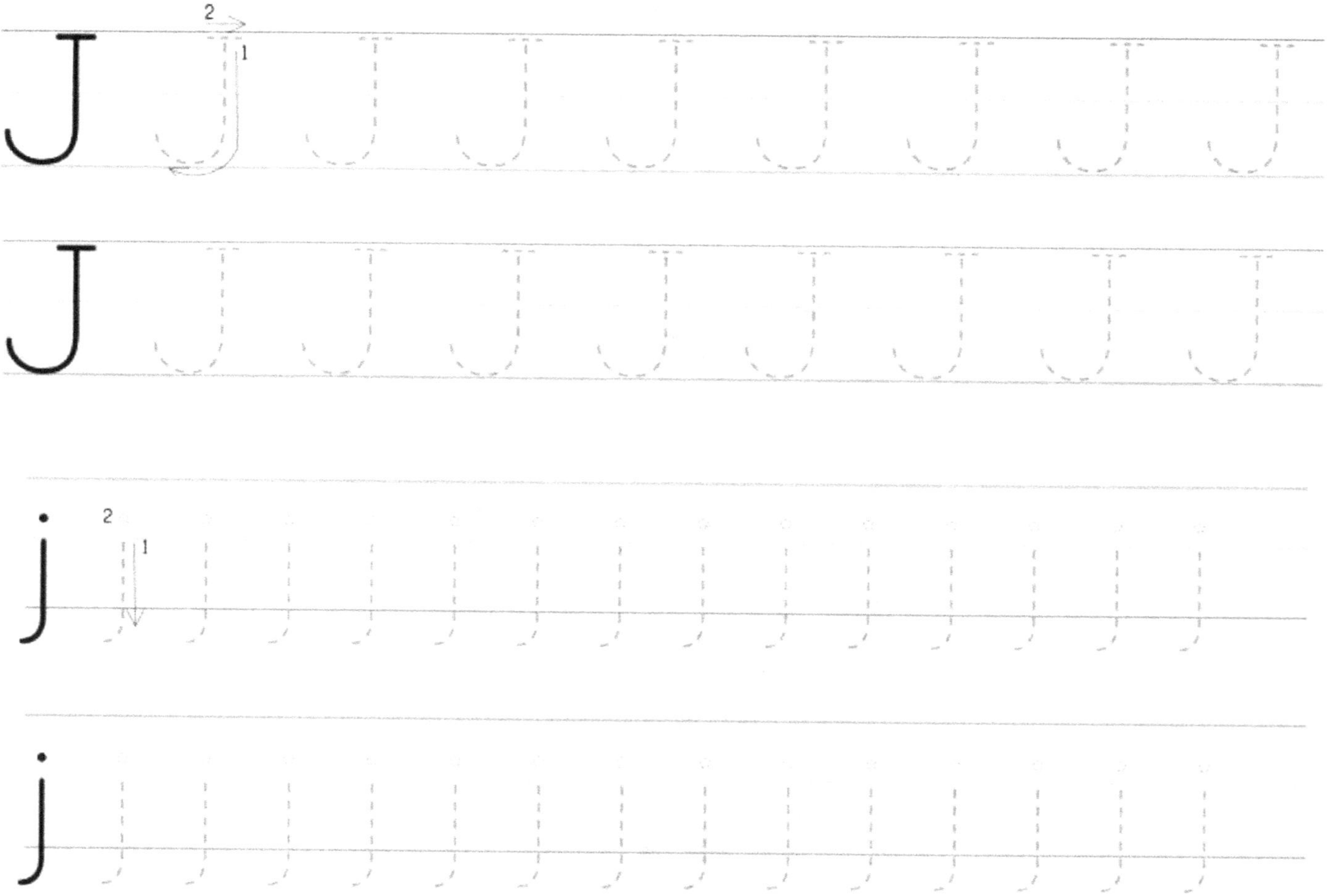

J J J J J J J J J J J

J J J J J J J J J J J

j j j j j j j j j j j

j j j j j j j j j j j

Jar _______________

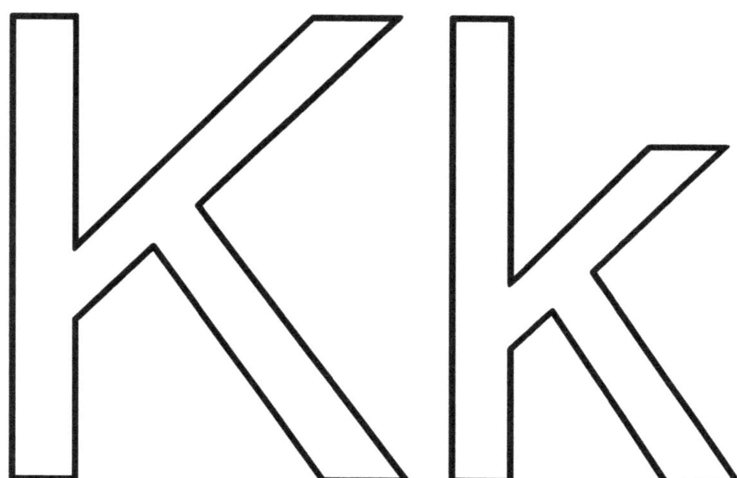

Trace the letters with a pencil

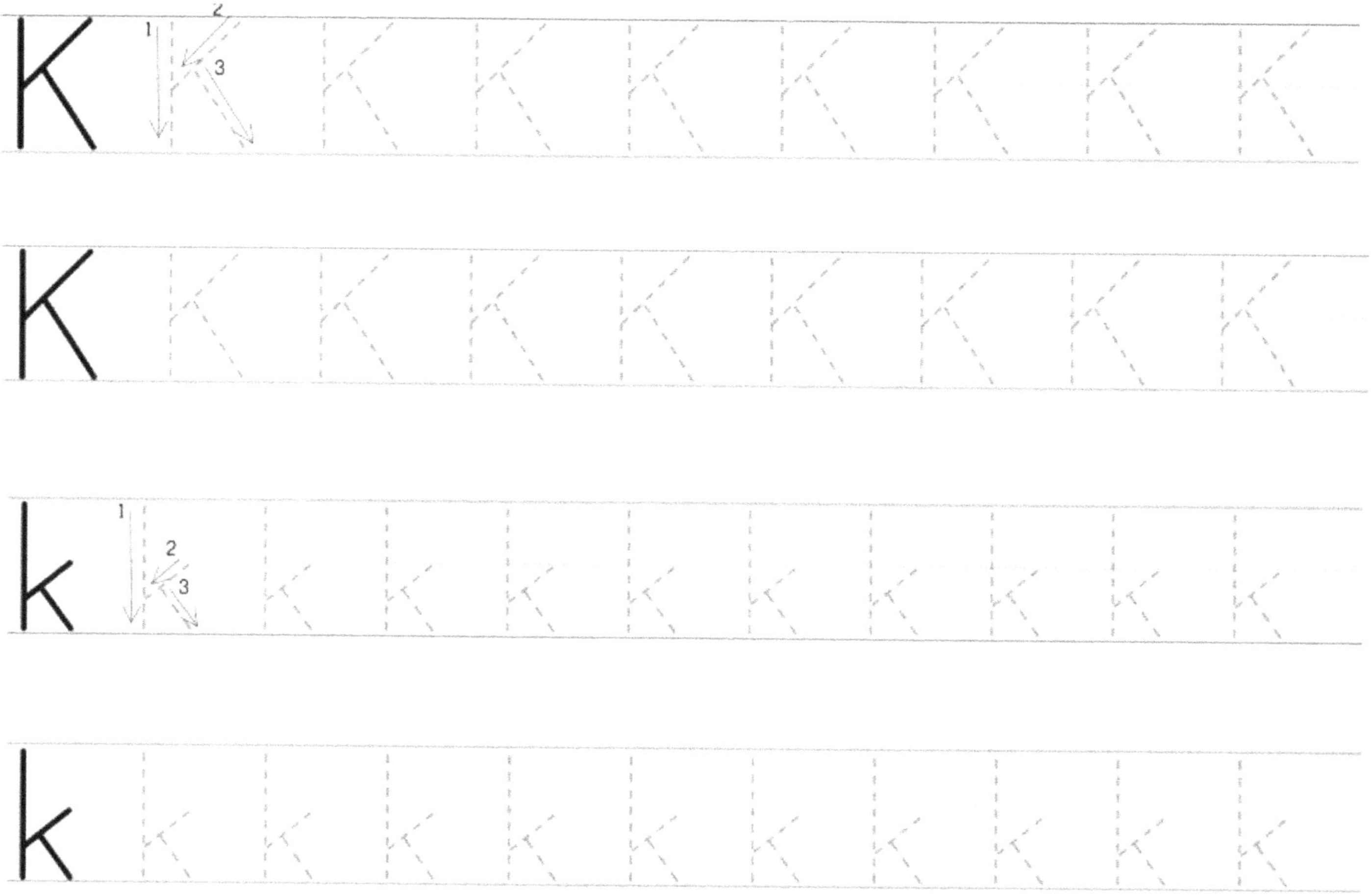

K

K

k

k

Kite _______________

L l

Trace the letters with a pencil

L

L

l

l

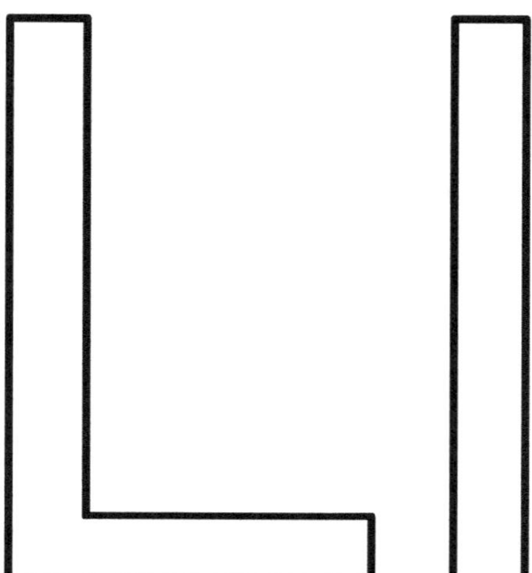

Lion

M

M

m

m

Monkey ＿＿＿＿＿＿＿

Nn

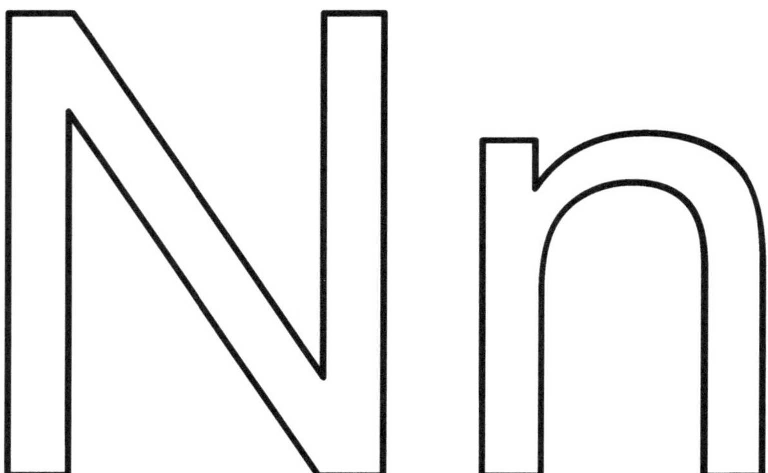

Trace the letters with a pencil

N

N

n

n

Nest ______________

Oo

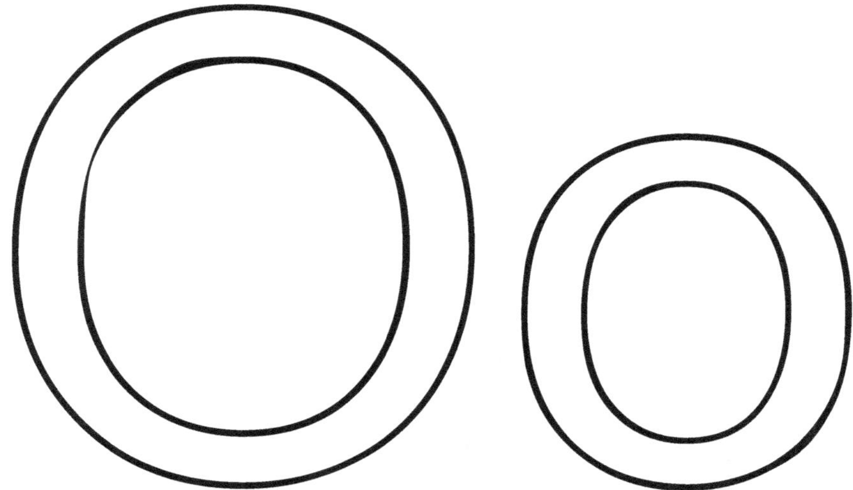

Trace the letters with a pencil

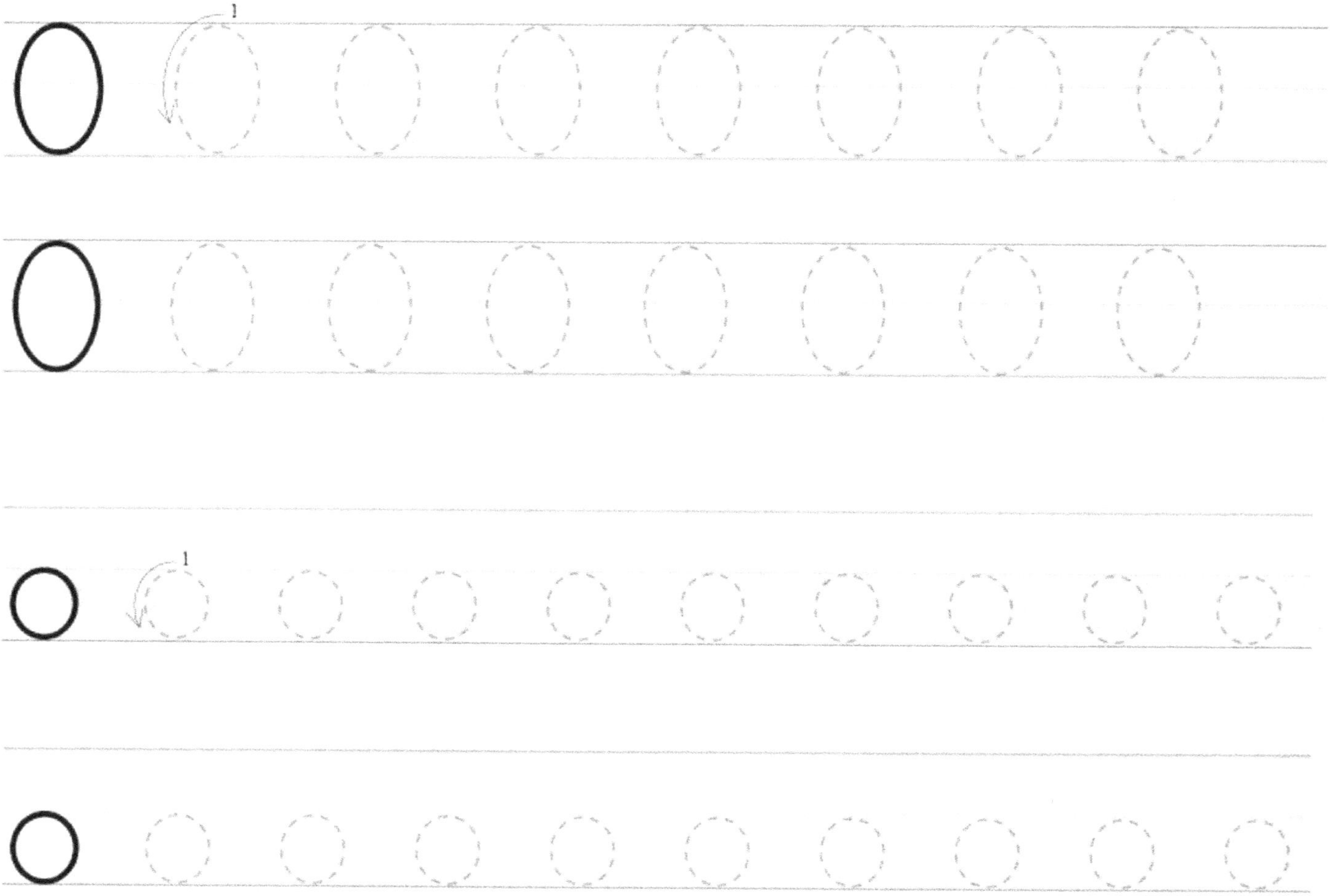

Owl ________________

Trace the letters with a pencil

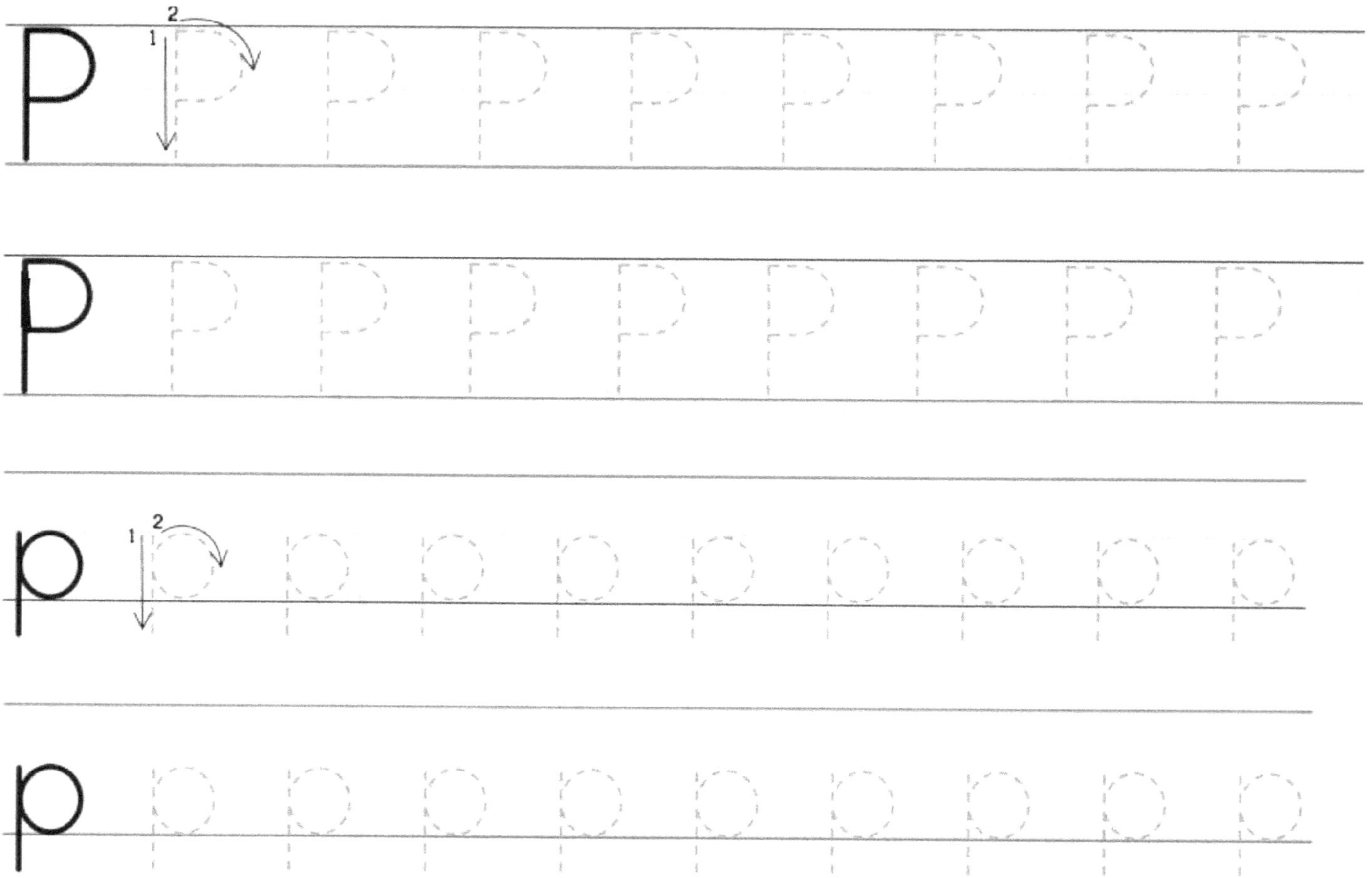

P P P P P P P P P P

P P P P P P P P P

p p p p p p p p p

p p p p p p p p p

Pineapple ———

Trace the letters with a pencil

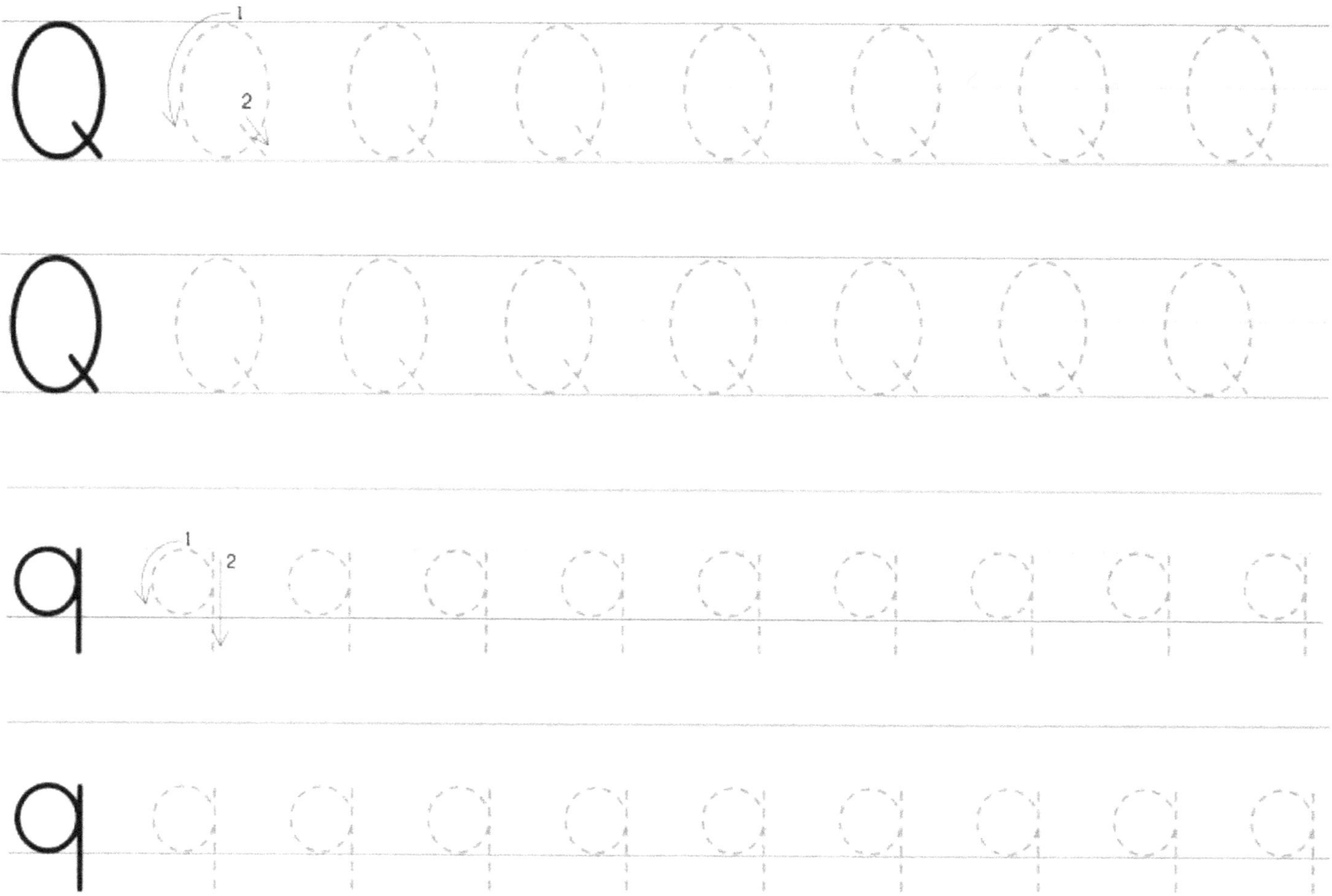

Queen ________

Trace the letters with a pencil

R

R

r

r

Rainbow ————

Ss

Trace the letters with a pencil

S

S

s

s

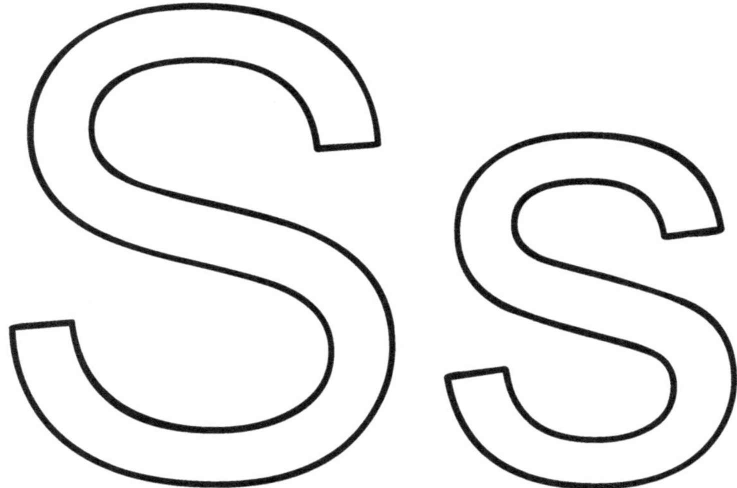

Snake ———————

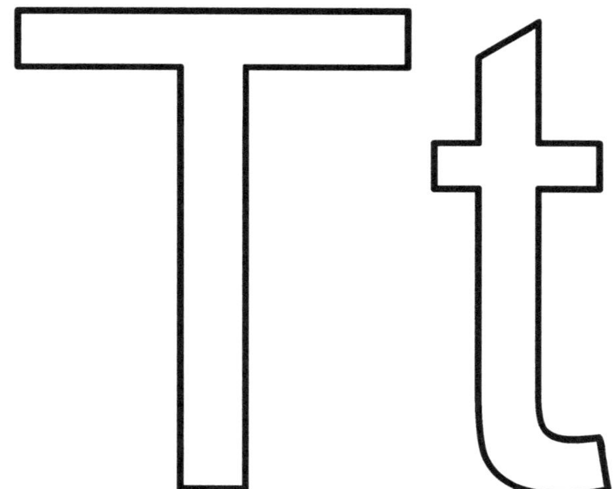

Trace the letters with a pencil

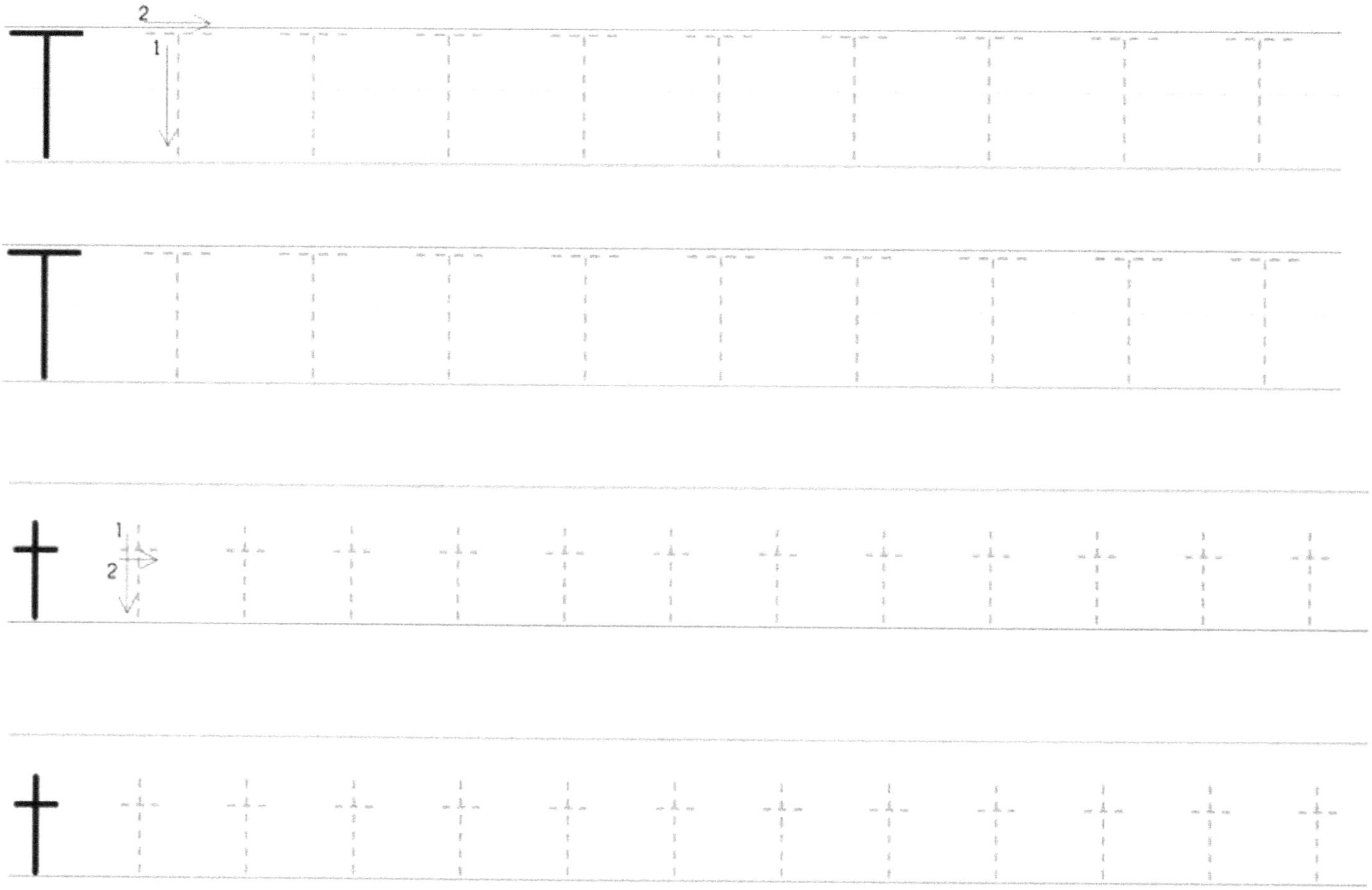

Turtle ___________

Uu

Trace the letters with a pencil

U

U

u

u

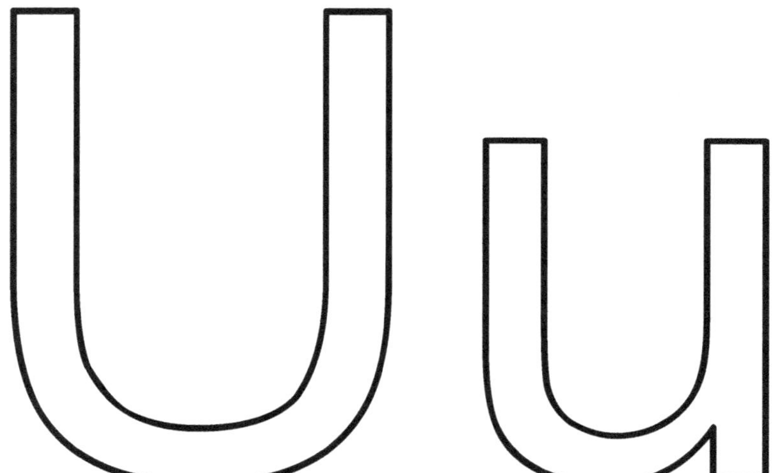

Umbrella ———

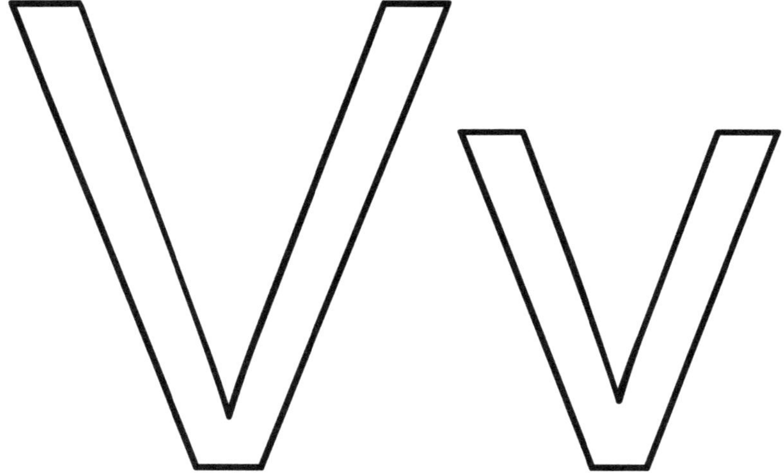

Trace the letters with a pencil

V
V
V
V

Violin ─────────────

Ww

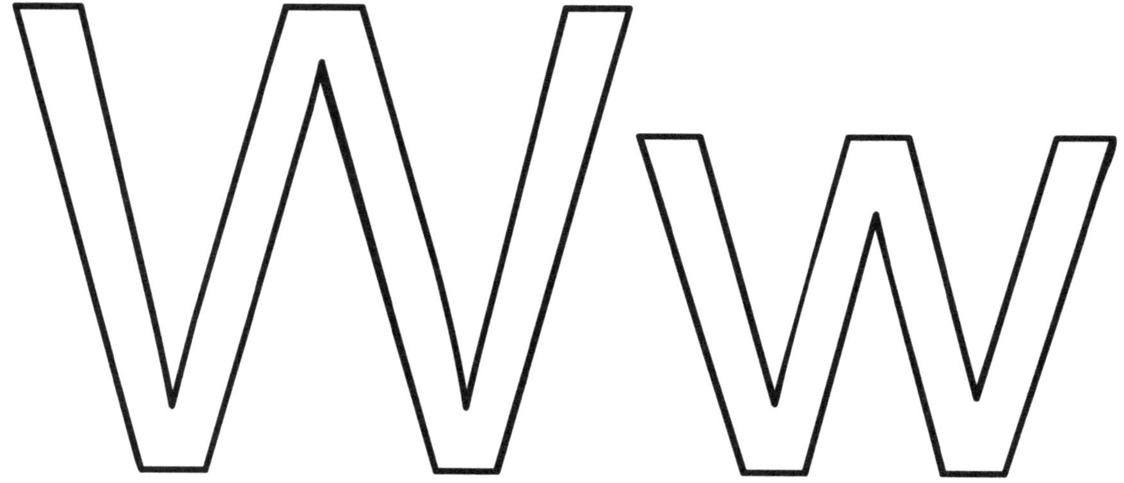

Trace the letters with a pencil

Whale _______________

Xx

Trace the letters with a pencil

X 1 2

X

x 1 2

x

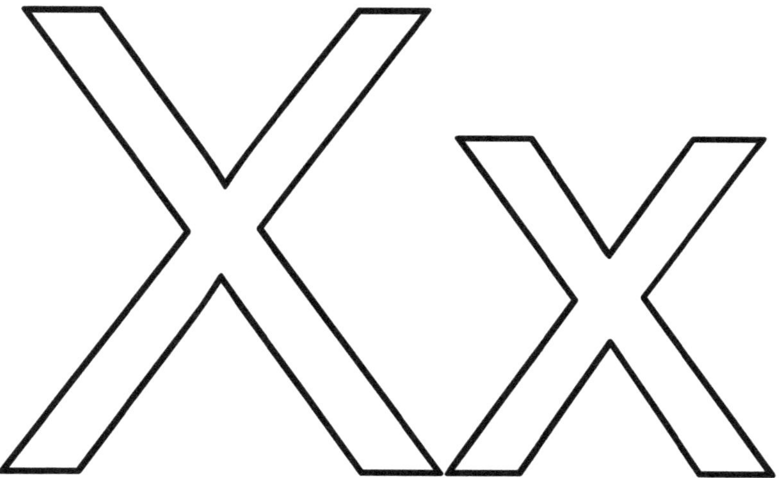

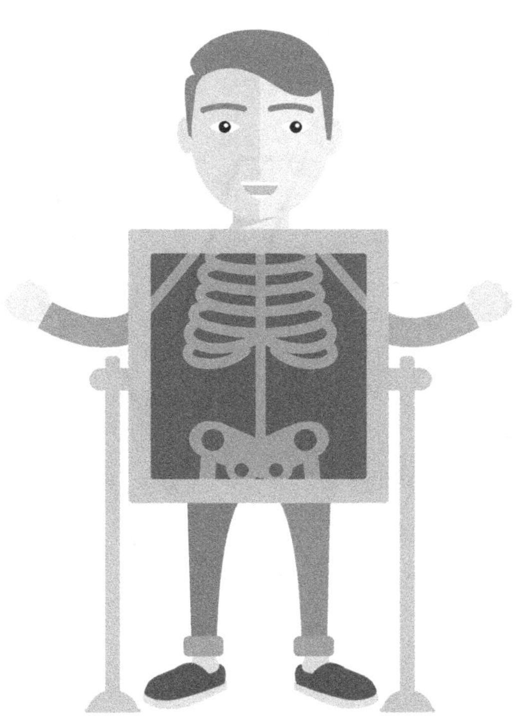

X-ray _________

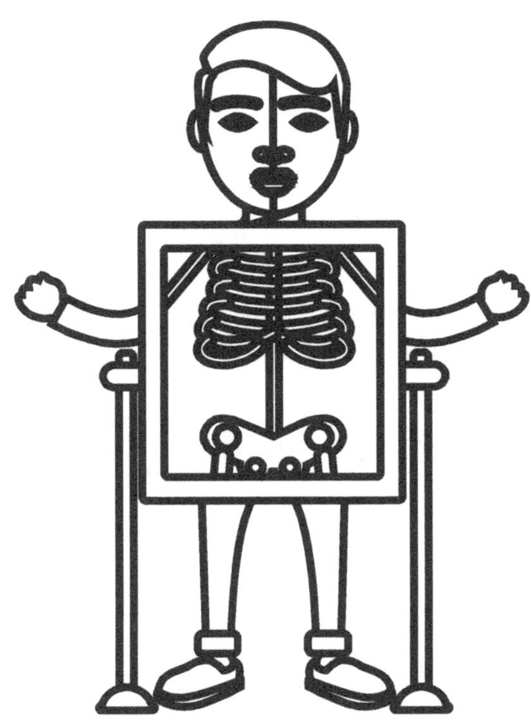

Yy

Trace the letters with a pencil

Y

Y

y

y

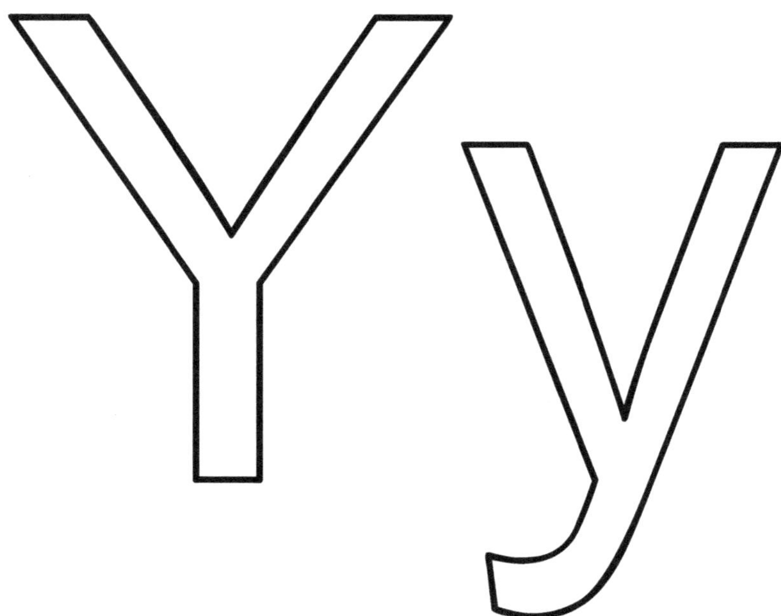

Yacht ─────────

Zz

Trace the letters with a pencil

Z

Z

z

z

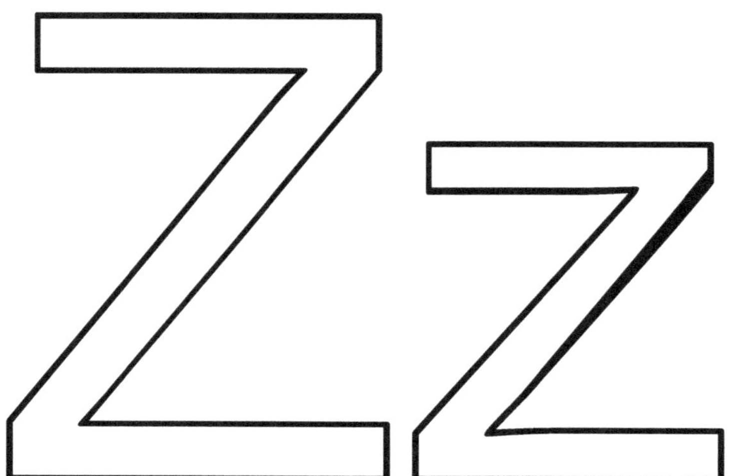

Zebra

2

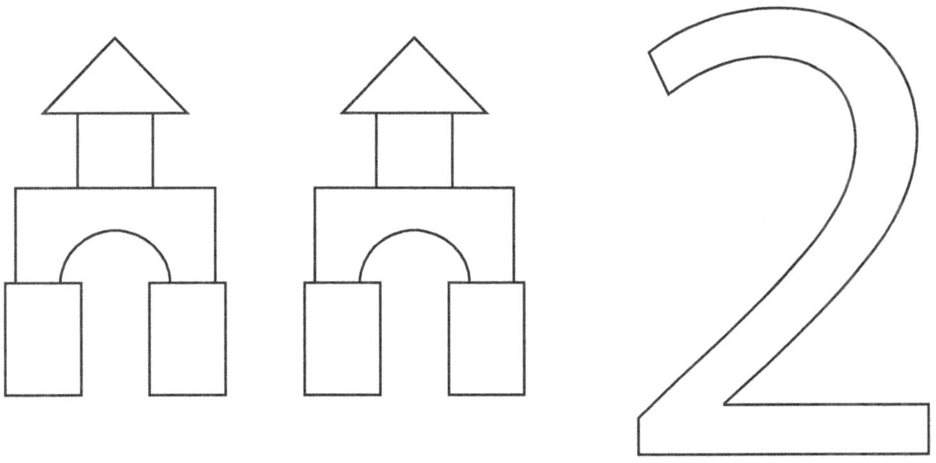

2

2

3

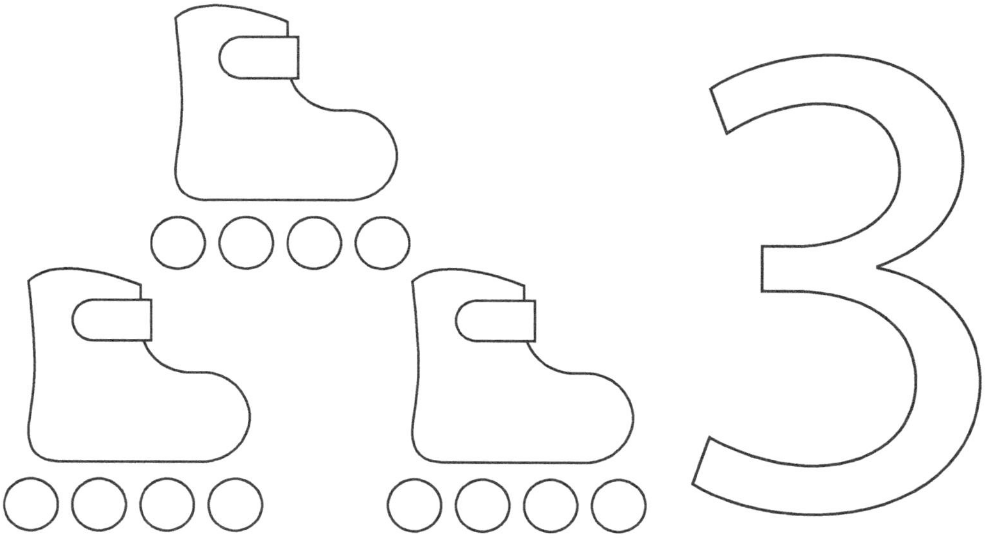

3

3

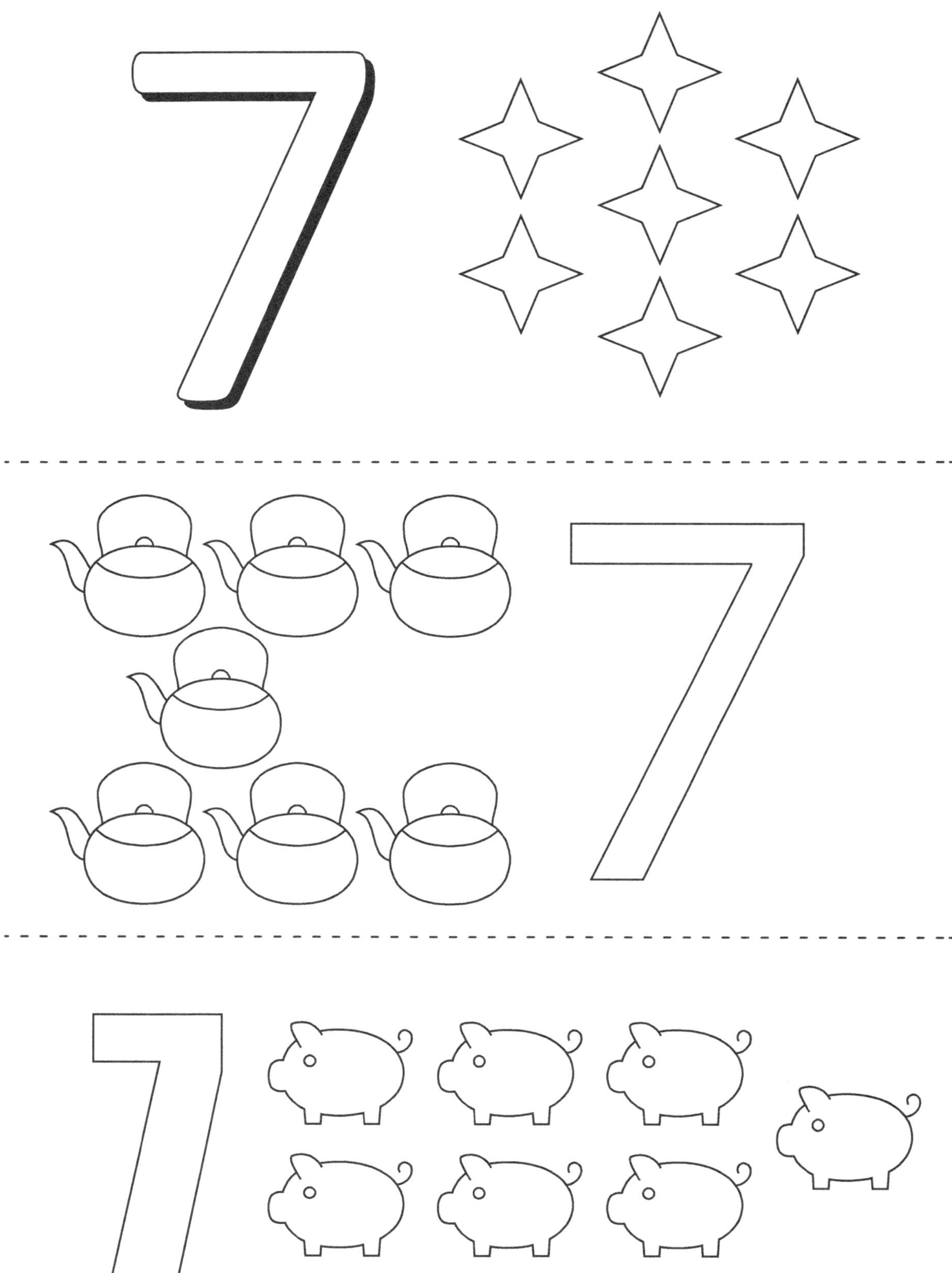

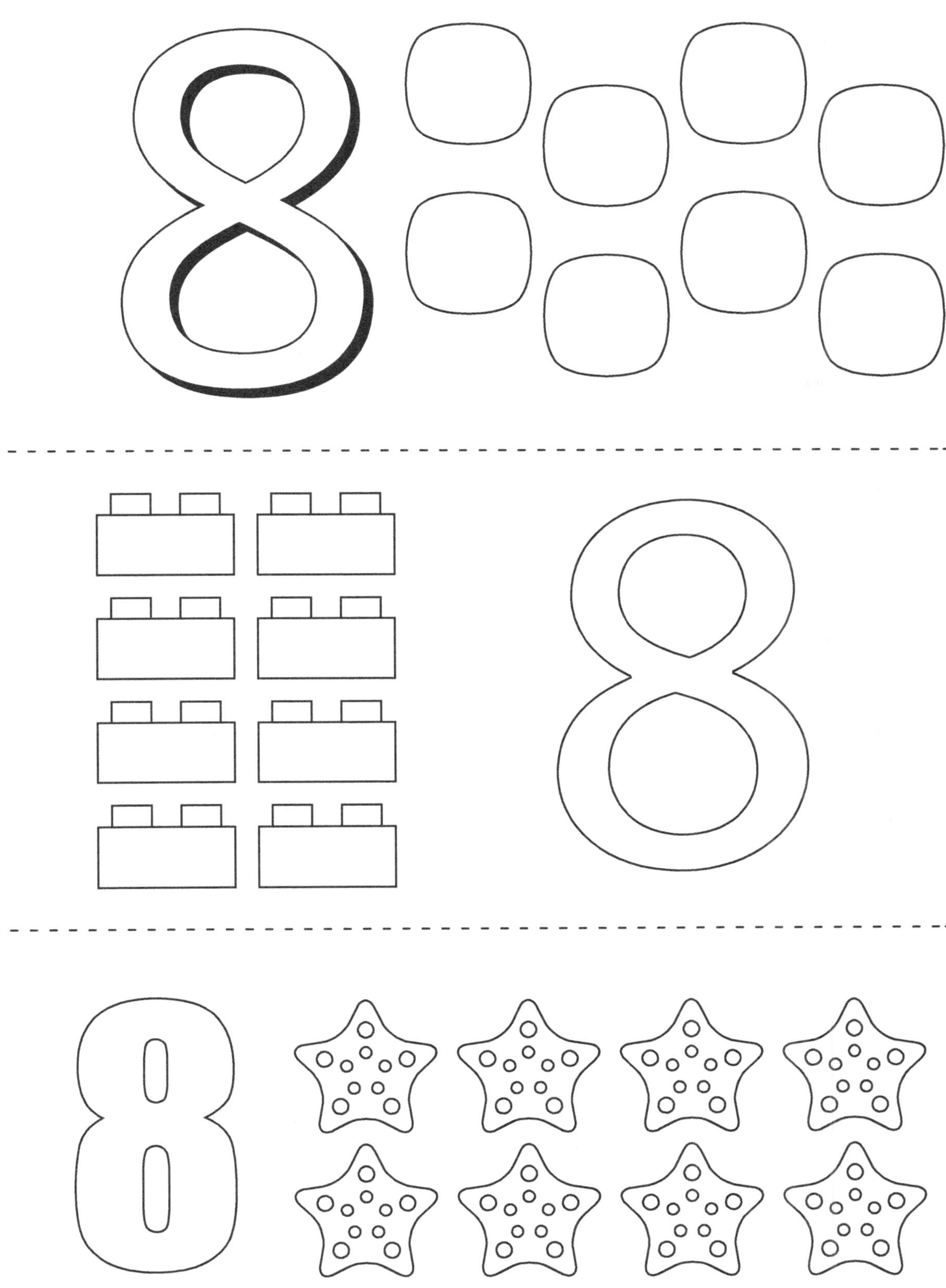

10

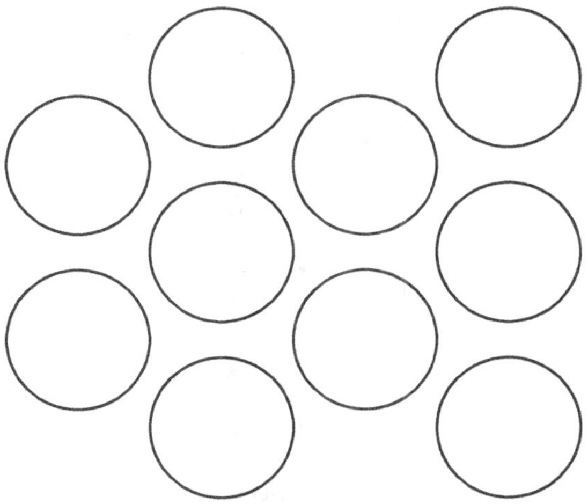

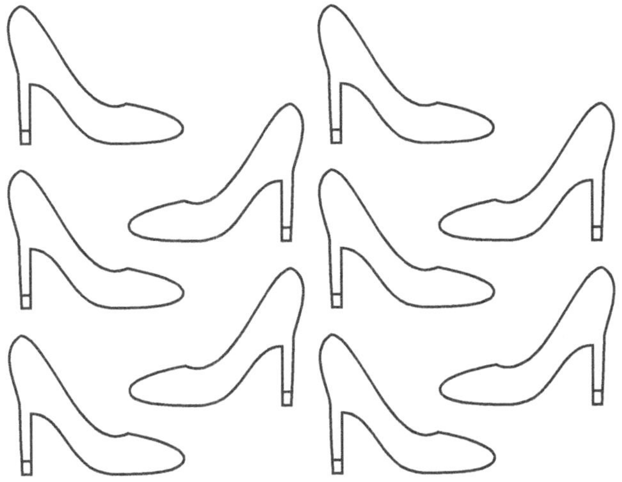

10

10

1   1

2 2

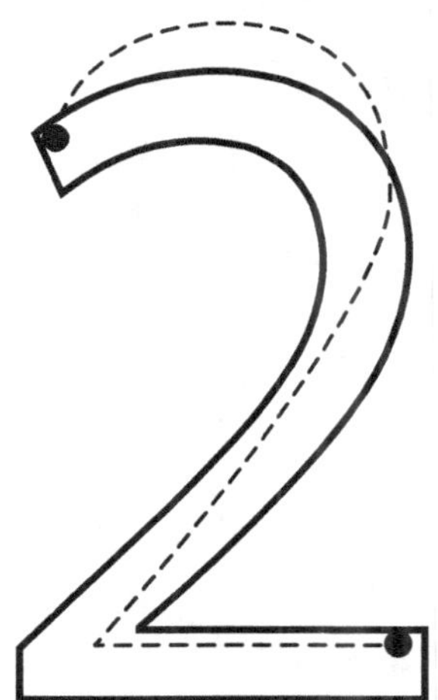

3   3

4

5 5

7 7

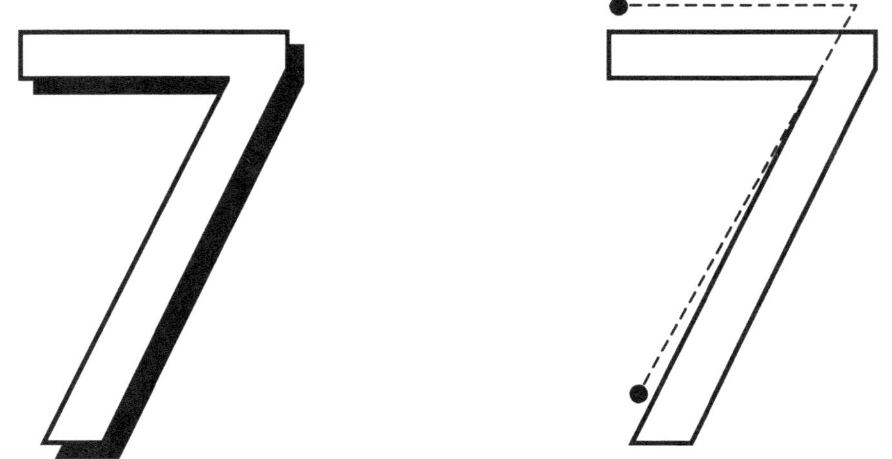

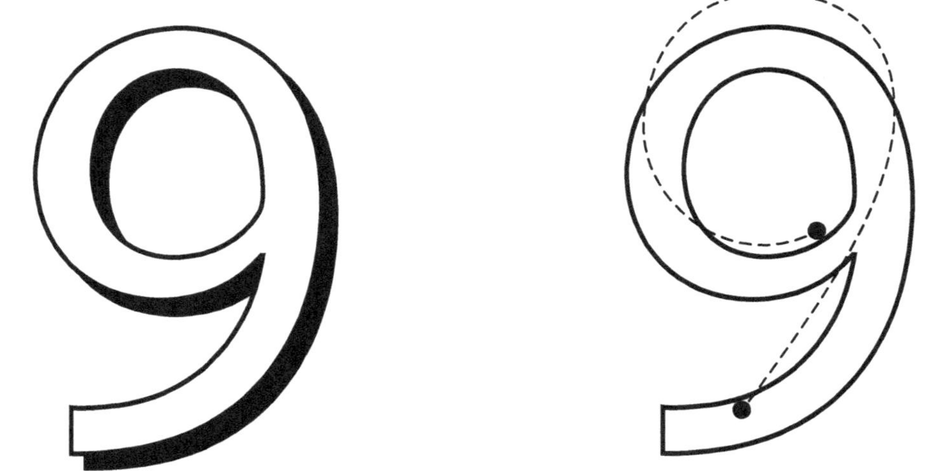

10 10

Aa Bb Cc Dd Ee
Ff Gg Hh Ii Jj Kk
Ll Mm Nn Oo Pp
Qq Rr Ss Tt Uu
Vv Ww Xx Yy Zz

Congratulations!

9 781797 595238